History of West Indies

History of West Indies

Aborigines and Physical Geography

Edith B. Blake - Felix L. Oswald

Part I

Aborigines of the West Indies[1]

Some little interest having again been awakened in the outside world concerning the West Indian Islands, the question is occasionally asked:

> Had those islands any aborigines when discovered by Europeans?
>
> If there were natives, do any of them remain?

Both questions may be answered in the affirmative.

The West Indies, or Antilles, consist of many hundreds, or even—reckoning keys or very small islands—several thousand islands varying in area from those which,

---

[1] By Edith Bernal Blake

like Cuba and Jamaica, number their square acres by the million, to the tiny key of half an acre or less. The greater number of these—indeed, all capable of supporting a population, with the exception of Barbados— contained inhabitants when first discovered. Barbados, though containing numerous evidences of former occupation, was uninhabited when taken possession of by its first European settlers, the English.

The peculiar interest attaching to the meeting between the European navigators and the Western barbarians is that—putting aside the discoveries of the Northmen in the tenth and eleventh centuries—it is the first meeting between modern and prehistoric man of which we have any account. Till the beginning of the nineteenth century the civilized world knew little or nothing of prehistoric man, and prehistoric anthropology was an unknown science. To have stated that man had existed on the earth more than four thousand years b. c. would have been regarded as heresy, and to have held that he had roamed over Europe when the mammoth crashed through its forests, and when the stately megaceros and reindeer browsed on its bogs, would have been considered the wildest folly. The stronger light that is being thrown on those times of long ago first shone in Denmark, where the study of runic stones and characters led to the disclosure of evidences of human occupation of that country far earlier than had ever heretofore been suspected. Subsequently, the finds at Abbeville, the discovery of the lake dwellings in Switzerland, the investigations in the caves of Kirkdale and Kent's Hole in England, with others too numerous to mention, awoke widespread interest in the newly arisen branch of investigation; learned men began to compare the remains and relics of the aborigines of America with those of Europe, and at length began to recognize that when Columbus landed on Guanahani, and was met by its painted and trembling inhabitants, the people of the Old World, instead of finding men of a new kind, were in reality standing face to face with men such as in Europe had been extinct for nigh two thousand years. This it is that gives such fascination to the descriptions left us by those who first saw men who were living very much as must have done the owners of the Cro-Magnon and Neanderthal skulls, and that lends such peculiar interest to all vestiges and traces that have been preserved of a people secluded from all contact with those more enlightened than themselves.

Fortunately, there is considerable material available for so interesting a study. Besides relics of the aborigines in the shape of skulls, bones, stone and wooden implements, and rock-carvings, some of which are more or less abundant in most of the islands, the early writers have left us graphic descriptions of these people, their manners and customs; and they give us the facts as they passed before their eyes, without any endeavor to bend such facts to the support of their own pet theory, or to explain what they did not understand, save by the usual and satisfactory method of assigning everything of which they disapproved or for which they could not account to the agency of the devil.

It is indeed fortunate that the discoverers have given us so many details of what they saw in those beautiful islands, which they flattered themselves were the outposts of the empire of the Great Khan, for the people they saw there have long since passed away, leaving no posterity behind them, save in the case of the Caribs of Dominica and St. Vincent. The Lucayans of the Bahamas, the Arrowauks of Cuba and the larger Antilles have for the last three hundred years or so been extinct. It is true that at Parottee Point, in Jamaica, a few of the fishermen claim to have Indian blood in their veins, and one old man assured me he was a pure Indian by descent. These people had straight black hair, and were decidedly different in feature to their negro neighbors. However, in all probability the Indian element is accounted for by Indians having not infrequently been brought to Jamaica either from the Mosquito coast or Florida. Sir Hans Sloane, who came to Jamaica more than two centuries ago as physician to the Duke of Albemarle, speaks of Indians there—

not natives of the island, they being all destroyed by the Spaniards, but are usually brought by surprise from the Mosquitos or from Florida, or such as were, slaves to the Spaniards and taken from them by the English. They are very good hunters and fishers, but are naught at working in the field or slavish work, and if checked or drubbed are good for nothing, therefore are very gently treated and well fed.

Curiously enough, at the present day the people claiming Indian descent in Jamaica are still expert fishermen.

I was informed by General Légitime, ex-President of Haiti, that in that island, in the wild, forest-clad mountains beyond

Jacmel, people live in the woods who never visit the towns or hold any communication with the present owners of the island, and who are believed to be descendants of the native Indians. It would be interesting if some communication with these people could be established, but meantime it is as likely they may be Maroons as Indians, for all concerning them is too vague and uncertain to allow at present of their being regarded as representatives of the aborigines.

In Dominica, St. Vincent, and Trinidad a few of the primitive inhabitants still remain. They are Caribs, who were a fierce and warlike race, the bitter enemies and persecutors of the comparatively mild and inoffensive Arrowauks. Both tribes still exist in Guiana, and apparently have forgotten their old differences. It is probable that the Arrowauks were the earliest arrivals in the islands, but when their migration from the mainland took place there are not sufficient data for saying: all we know is that it must have been long ages before the arrival of the Europeans. In Hispaniola (now the negro republics of Haiti and Santo Domingo) the absence of any legend of a distant origin would allow of the native Indians having had a legitimate claim to being an autochthonous race, or at any rate points to the great length of time that must have passed since their canoes had carried them across the breezy Caribbean Sea, from the cradle of their race far away in the dense and mysterious forests of South America. The Indians of Hispaniola, like many others of their brethren, handed down their histories and traditions in songs which were chanted before the people on festivals and other great occasions, and which were often accompanied by dances. On great occasions they danced to the sound of a drum made out of the trunk of a tree and played by a cacique. In these songs or hymns the tradition was recorded that the first men came out of two caverns in the island. The sun was irritated at the advent of mankind, so changed the guardians of the caves into stones, and metamorphosed the men who had escaped from the caves into trees, frogs, and different animals. In spite, however, of these efforts on the part of the great luminary, the world became peopled. Another tradition declared that the sun and moon themselves had come out of a cavern in Haiti.

The traditions of the Lucayans, on the contrary, all pointed to the Lucayans having come to those islands from a land to the south, so probably their residence in the Bahamas had not been for so long a period as to blot out all recollection of the large islands where their race had struck such firm root on its migration from the mainland. That the Arrowauk occupation of the islands had been of long duration, a mass of evidence appears to show. In Cuba artificially flattened skulls have been discovered imbedded in lime rock in caves near Cape Maisi. With them were found fragments of pottery, an earthen jar containing bones, and some stone axes or celts, popularly known as "thunderbolts." In Jamaica we ourselves found pottery and bones imbedded in a cave in the rocks, out of which we had to break them with a machete, or cutlass. In the Jamaica cave, however, the lime in which the bones were incrusted appeared to be of stalactitic nature, and may have been deposited more rapidly than would have been the formation of true limestone. The district in which the cave is situated (the St. John's Hills, Guanaboa) is a very dry one, and there was no appearance of any drip from the roof or sides of the cave when we visited it; so it may be assumed that the incrustation must, in any case, have been a slow process. The Indians had been exterminated in Jamaica for a considerable period before its occupation by the English, which took place in the days of Cromwell, so even a low computation of the lapse of time must assign a respectable antiquity to the incrusted pottery and bones. When more extensive researches and explorations take place, it is possible that traces of human presence may be discovered in some of the older rocks or strata of some of the islands.

That all the larger islands were inhabited by a race which was divided into tribes, some of which spoke different dialects, but which derived their origin from the same stock, is shown not alone from evidence afforded by skulls, pottery, and implements, but from the fact of identity of language. On Columbus's first voyage he carried home with him some of the natives to exhibit in Spain. Among these was a boy named Didacus, taken by the admiral from Guanahani, now generally known as Watling's Island, the scene of the landfall. We are told that Didacus "was a man from his child's age, brought up with the admiral." Later on he sailed with Columbus back to the Antilles and acted as his interpreter, and eventually Guarionexius, the King of Cibana (in Hispaniola), in order to secure to himself the friendship of

Columbus, gave his sister as wife to Didacus. In most of the islands Didacus appears to have understood the language with ease, and when he failed to do so the fact is expressly stated. This was the case at one end of Cuba.

> But here [writes the old chronicler] Didacus, the interpreter, which understood the language of the beginning of Cuba, understood not them one whit; whereby they [the Spaniards] considered that in many provinces of Cuba were sundry languages.

Who these people were whose tongue was incomprehensible to a Lucayan, who spoke the Arrowauk language, we have no means of judging. As Didacus could not understand these people "one whit," the difference in their tongue from that of the generality of the Arrowauk descendants must have been very great, more so apparently than that of a diversity of *patois* or of accent. This seems to point to the fact that there were other Indians living in some of the islands besides Arrowauks and Caribs. We know that from time to time Indian traders from the mainland visited the islands, and some of them may have remained and settled in them. On his fourth voyage Columbus met some of these trading canoes, and Peter Martyr gives a detailed account of the event from a letter written by Columbus himself.

> Leaving the islands of Cuba and Jamaica on his right hand toward the north, he [Columbus] writeth that he chanced upon an island more southward than Jamaica, which the inhabitants call Guamassa, so flourishing and fruitful that it might seem an earthly paradise. Coasting along by the shores of this island, he met two of the canoes or boats of those provinces, which were drawn of two naked slaves against the stream. In

these boats were carried a ruler of the island, with his wife and children, all naked. The slaves, seeing our men aland, made signs to them to stand out of the way, and threatened them if they would not give place. Their simpleness is such that they neither feared the multitude or power of our men, or the greatness and strangeness of our ships. They thought that our men would have honored their master with like reverence as they did. Our men had intelligence at the length that this ruler was a great merchant, which came to the mart from other coasts of the island, for they exercise buying and selling by exchange with their confines. He had also with him good store of such ware as they stand in need of, or take pleasure in: as laton bells, razors, knives, and hatchets, made of a certain sharp yellow stone, with handles of a strong kind of wood; also many other necessary instruments, with kitchen stuff, and vessels for all necessary uses; likewise sheets of gossampine cotton, wrought of sundry colors. Our men took him prisoner, with all his family, but Columbus commanded him to be loosed shortly after, and the greatest part of his goods to be restored to win his friendship.

The Arrowauks were ignorant of the working of metals, so the mention of "laton bells" as part of the stock in trade of this roving trader points to his having come from the mainland, where the Zuñis, Aztecs, Mayas, and Peruvians were all workers of bronze, or laton, though they had not progressed so far as the use of iron.

That the Caribs were later comers in the Antilles than the Arrowauks seems likely from the fact that they had only established themselves in the smaller islands, and made thence raids on the inhabitants of the larger ones; for it is highly improbable that, had so fierce and domineering a people had time to increase and multiply, they would have left their weaker neighbors in possession of all the larger islands, though it is possible they regarded the latter as stock farms whence to draw supplies for their larders. Some authors even assert that the arrival of Caribs in the islands could only have shortly preceded the Columban discovery. The Spaniards were astonished to observe that the Carib women spoke a different language from the men. The Caribs did not kill or eat the women whose tribes they attacked. The young women, says Martyr, "they take to keep for increase, as we do hens to lay eggs; the old women they make their drudges." Alluding to this fact, and discussing the probable date of the arrival of the Caribs in the West Indian Archipelago, Dr. D. G. Brinton says:

> The latter event was then of such recent occurrence that the women of the island

> Caribs, most of whom had been captured from Arowaks, *still spoke that tongue.*

The comparatively mild and inoffensive Arrowauks must have had a bad time of it when the Caribs were on the war path in those lovely islands, about which Martyr writes so enthusiastically as "an earthly paradise," where

> was never any noisome beast found in it, nor yet any ravening four-footed beast: no lion, no bear, no fierce tygers, no crafty foxes, nor devouring wolves. All things are blessed and fortunate,

exclaims he, writing of Hispaniola; but the human enemy, more relentless and deadly than four-footed beast, must have been a blighting factor in the happiness of the daily life of the Arrowauk, even before the arrival of Spanish oppressors. "They of the islands," writes the old monk, ignoring his having pronounced all things there "blessed and fortunate,"

when they perceive the cannibals coming have no other shift but only to flee, for although they use very sharp arrows made of reeds, yet are they of small force to repress the fury of the cannibals, for even they themselves confess that ten of the cannibals are able to overcome a hundred of them if they encounter with them.

Cruel as were the Spaniards to the unfortunate Indians in general, to the Arrowauks they must at first have appeared almost as benefactors compared to the Caribs, and indeed the more severe enactments of the conquerors were avowedly directed against those Indians "guilty of that unnatural crime" of eating human flesh.

Nowadays that travelers in Africa, New Zealand, the Pacific, and elsewhere have made us familiar with stories of cannibalism as a widespread practice among savage peoples, and that research has shown us that in prehistoric times it may not have been unknown even in Europe, we often fail to appreciate the horror and astonishment with which so strange and revolting a habit filled the early Spanish navigators. It came upon them as a shock, a horror which was a novelty, and therefore all the more abominable. We are always apt to overlook cruelties and evils with which we are familiar, while rarely failing to be scandalized at those that are new to us. The Spaniards were not squeamish about cruelty, and indeed the word cannot be applied to cannibalism, for once a man is dead it is not more cruel to eat his body than to bury or burn it.

The Inquisition had made the Spaniards callous to barbarity, but cannibalism was a different matter; they were not accustomed to it, had never before met with it. Rough sailors, relentless bigots as they were, who at home doubtless would have attended a bullfight or an *auto-da-fe* with equal pleasure, they could not stomach cannibalism, and it was with loathing and unspeakable disgust that in the round, bell-like houses of an Indian village they often found

in their kitchens man's flesh, duck's flesh, and goose flesh, all in one pot, and other on the spits ready to be laid on the fire. Entering into their inner lodgings, they found fagots of the bones of men's arms and legs, which they reserve to make heads for their arrows, because they lack iron; the other bones they cast away when they have eaten the flesh. They found likewise the head of a young man fastened to a post, and yet bleeding.

By the people supposed to be of Arrowauk descent the Spaniards were generally received with submission and fear, the people mistaking them for Caribs, except in a part of Jamaica, where the inhabitants at first offered a feeble resistance. In some instances the new arrivals were even worshiped as gods. Such was the case in the Bahamas and in Haiti, where ancient prophecies had taught the Indians to expect the arrival of Maguacochios — i. e., men clothed in apparel, and armed with such swords as should cut a man in sunder at one stroke, under whose yoke their posterity should be subdued.

The existence of these prophecies seems not to have excited any great surprise or to have caused much speculation as to their origin in the minds of the Spaniards.

Such apparently miraculous foresight on the part of the Indians the new arrivals easily, and to themselves satisfactorily, accounted for by the fact that the barbarians were worshipers of the Evil One, and that their priests and idols, or zemis, were enabled to prophesy because of their intercourse and familiarity with devils. But, notwithstanding much that was objectionable and false, the creed of the Indians does not appear to have been altogether debased, and as explained to Columbus by one of the old chieftains of Cuba, the doctrines of those remote and benighted savages might claim some affinity to those professed by the Christians. Columbus and his men had landed and were hearing mass on the Cuban shore when "there came toward him a certain governor, a man of fourscore years of age, and of great gravity, although he were naked," and who had a great train of men waiting on him. All the while the priest was at mass he showed himself very humble, and gave reverent attendance with grave and demure countenance.

When mass was over the old chief "presented to the admiral a casket of the fruits of his country, delivering the same with his own hands."

After Columbus had "gently entertained him," the old man made a speech, which Didacus, the interpreter, translated to the Spaniards to the following effect:

> I have been advertised (most mighty prince) that you have of late with great power subdued many lands and regions hitherto unknown to you, and have brought no little fear upon all the people and inhabitants of the same: the which your good fortune you shall bear with less insolency, if you remember that the souls of men have two

journeys after they are departed from this body. The one, foul and dark, prepared for such as are injurious and cruel to mankind; the other, pleasant and delectable, ordained for them which in their lifetime loved peace and quietness. If therefore you acknowledge yourself to be mortal, and consider that every man shall receive condign reward or punishment for such things as he hath done in this life, you will wrongfully hurt no man.

Columbus, marveling at the judgment of the naked old man, answered that he was glad to hear his opinion as touching the sundry journeys and rewards of souls departed from the bodies, supposing that neither he or any other of the inhabitants of those regions had had any knowledge thereof; declaring further that the chief cause of his coming thither was to instruct them in such godly knowledge and true religion . . . and especially to subdue and punish the cannibals and such other mischievous people, and to defend innocents against the violence of evildoers, etc.

The old man was so pleased with these comfortable words of the admiral that he became desirous of forsaking Cuba and accompanying Columbus to Spain, "notwithstanding his extreme age," and was with difficulty deterred from the purpose by his wife and children, who fell prostrate at the feet of the old cacique, imploring him with tears not to forsake and leave them desolate.

At whose pitiful requests the worthy old man, being moved, remained at home, to the comfort of his people and family, satisfying rather them than himself; for, not yet ceasing to wonder, and of heavy countenance because he might not depart, he demanded oftentimes if that land was not heaven which brought forth such men.

The Caribs were of different mettle from the inhabitants of the larger islands. They resisted to their utmost, and sometimes, without waiting to be assailed, attacked the Spaniards even at sea. In the Gulf of Paria we read that the Spanish vessels met with a navy of eighteen canoes of cannibals, which went a-roving to hunt for men, who, as soon as they had espied our men, assailed their ship (that of Petrus Alphonsus, called Uignus) fiercely, and without fear inclosed the same, disturbing our men on every side with their arrows.

But, courageous as they were, the novel terror of the flash and smoke and thunder of the guns struck consternation into the daring cannibals, who turned and fled before the unexpected and alarming fire and fury of the cannon. The Spaniards gave chase and captured one of the canoes; in it was only one Carib; his companion or companions had escaped, but in the piragua lay a captive tied and bound, who, with tears running down his cheeks, made the Spaniards understand by gestures that six of his comrades had already been killed and eaten, and that such was to have been his own fate on the following day. The Spaniards unbound the prisoner and gave him power over the cannibal to do with him what he would. Then, with the cannibal's own club, he laid on him all that he might drive hand and foot, grieving and fretting as it had been a wild boar, thinking that he had not yet sufficiently revenged the death of his companions when he had beaten out the brains and guts.

Speaking of the Caribs of the mainland, the old writer says: "That wild kind of men, dispersed through the large distance of those coasts, hath sometimes slain whole armies of the Spaniards." Indeed, the Caribs even mocked at their invaders, designating them as women or children, in ridicule of their white teeth, those of the Caribs "being black as coals, from a leaf they chewed."

The Arrowauks were taller than the Caribs, but not so robust, in color of a clear brown, their complexion, according to Columbus, not being much darker than that of a Spanish peasant. Both Arrowauks and Caribs flattened their heads, though each race had a different fashion of doing so.

By this practice [says Herrera] the crown was so strengthened that a Spanish broadsword, instead of cleaving the skull at a stroke, would frequently break short upon it.

Various reasons have been assigned for the singular fashion of flattening the head that obtained throughout the Antilles. It is said that infants whose heads are so treated do not cry or moan as do babies whose heads are left to Nature; but if, as some anatomists affirm, the coronal sutures in the heads of infants born in the West Indies are exceptionally open, the strengthening of the skull was probably the reason that had originally brought flattened foreheads into fashion. The practice, it is believed, does not lessen the intelligence of the bearer of the flattened head, and if it has any effect on the brain it would be in the direction of subduing "speculative and emotional energy," while developing activity of limb. Their hair, like that of

Indians in general, was straight, coarse, and black; their features were hard and ugly; they had broad faces and flat noses, but their eyes showed great good nature, and their countenances were open and pleasing.

It was an honest face [says Martyr], coarse but not gloomy, for it was enlivened by confidence and softened by compassion.

Their wants were few, and sea and land furnished them with the necessaries of life, without exacting any severe or continuous labor on their part; so, as is almost invariably the case with natives of the tropics, the Arrowauks were indolent and indisposed to hard work, though showing considerable energy in their amusements, as we are told that "it was their custom to dance from evening to dawn." Another of their favorite pastimes was the game of *bato*, said somewhat to have resembled cricket. The players were divided into two sides, which alternately changed places. The ball with which they played was made of India rubber from the native milk withy, and the elastic nature of the material was a surprise to the Spaniards, who heretofore had not seen India rubber. Both men and women took part in the game; the ball was not caught with the hand, but received on head, elbow, or foot, and repelled with great force and dexterity. Wrestling and running for prizes were also well-known amusements among these people.

The great defect of the Arrowauks was their extreme immorality. Some of their dances were exceedingly indecent and disgusting, and the more abandoned a woman was, the greater was the consideration in which she was held. The religions and beliefs of the Indians varied more or less with the different tribes and races among them, and no doubt the Arrowauks had a variety of sects and formulas in the different islands. In broad lines we gather that they believed in a supreme being called Jocahuma, who had a father and mother residing sometimes in the sun and sometimes in the moon. Divine honors were also paid to images of wood, stone, and cotton, called zemis, which represented usually distorted versions of the human face and sometimes reptiles. A consecrated hut or temple was set apart in every village for worsip of these zemis, but only the priests or Bohitos were permitted to enter these temples, and they acted as intercessors for the people, besides practicing the art of medicine and superintending the education of the children of caciques and men of high rank. When the will of the cacique had received the approval of the Bohito or priest, it was received by the people as the decree of Heaven.

The spirits of the good were believed to go to a pleasant valley called Cozaba. There, surrounded by leafy trees laden with delicious fruits, the islanders looked forward to rejoining the spirits of their ancestors, and in cool shade beside flowing rivulets to rejoice in the society of the friends they had loved in the islands of earth, in a land where there were no hurricanes, no drought, and no Caribs. Each tribe appears to have considered that this paradise was situated in some mysterious way within their own province. During the day the souls of the departed hid themselves in the fastnesses of the mountains, but in the soft, fragrant tropical nights the souls were said to emerge from their retreat and to come down to the valley, to feed upon the fruit of the glossy-leaved mammee. This tree was consequently deemed sacred by the Indians, who refrained from eating the fruit lest the spirits of their ancestors might want food.

Of course, there were many variations in the rituals and beliefs of the religions of the various tribes. It would be as impossible to attempt an account even pretending to be comprehensive of their creed, in the space of a few pages, as it would be to do so of the churches and sects of Christianity; but such, in broad lines, is the sketch left us by the Spanish writers of the faith of the peoples of the Greater Antilles. Accounts of creeds given by opponents of the religion are, of course, always liable to misconceptions and perversions. The Indians, on their side, seem often to have been under the impression that the object worshiped and invoked by the Spaniards was gold, and not the Trinity. Gold they already regarded with a certain reverence, apparently esteeming it a sacred thing, as before setting out to seek for it they underwent a certain course of abstinence and fasting.

Hatuey, a cacique of Santo Domingo, had emigrated thence with his people to Cuba, in order to escape from the tyranny of the Europeans. The Spaniards pursued the fugitives, and the cacique exhorted his followers to resist to the uttermost, but pointed out to them that no bravery of theirs could prevail unless they invoked and conciliated the god of the Spaniards, who had shown himself to be so powerful, and in whose honor their enemies were ready to embark on any enterprise.

Behold him [exclaimed Hatuey, showing his men a basketful of gold], behold that god for whom they undertake so much; it is for him they came here. Let us, then, celebrate a feast in his honor, to obtain his protection.

Thereupon the Indians began their sacred songs, all the while dancing around the gold. Hatuey, however, declared that they could not be safe so long as the god of the Spaniards remained in their neighborhood, and that he should be buried where he could never be discovered. Amid shouts of joy from the people the gold was then cast into the sea. But, unfortunately for the Indians, his power was not so easily allayed as that of their zemis. The Spaniards came, the cacique fell into their hands, and was condemned to be burned alive. As he was being tied to the stake a Franciscan friar drew near and attempted his conversion, telling Hatuey of the heaven and hell of the Christians. "In this place of happiness whereof you speak," said the cacique, "are there any Spaniards?" "Assuredly," answered the missionary, "but only good ones." "The best of them were good for nothing," replied Hatuey, "and I desire not to go where I may be in danger of meeting with one of that horrid tribe."

"Les grands mangeurs de viande sont en général cruels et féroces, plus que les autres hommes; cette observation est de tous les lieux", (*The great eaters of meat are often cruel and ferocious, more than other men; this observation is real in all places)*" writes Rousseau, and the difference in the disposition of the Arrowauks and Caribs bears out the truth of the remark. The Arrowauks had little animal food, with the exception of fish, a few birds, reptiles, and insects; but the Carib larders were kept well furnished with human flesh, and even if an expedition had failed to bring back men prisoners for the table (women were not eaten), they had preserves of children taken in former raids, and fattened up till they were plump enough to be irresistible to any cannibal palate.

But though on festival occasions they no doubt gorged themselves both with meat and drink, as a rule, like Indians in general, they were very abstemious. Indeed, the Spaniards, although the most abstemious of Europeans, to the Indians—"whose abstemiousness," says an old writer, "exceeded that of the most mortified hermit"—appeared excessively voracious.

So surprised were they at the appetites of the Spaniards—one of whom was supposed to consume as much as ten Indians—that the islanders were of opinion that the Spaniards must have come among them in quest of food, their own country not producing enough to satisfy such immoderate appetites—a conclusion which Carib manners and customs would certainly assist in forming.

Both Arrowauks and Caribs were fond of smoking. They intoxicated themselves with tobacco, which they called cohiba, drawing up the fumes by a tube through the nostrils. A dream coming during the ensuing intoxication was regarded as an inspiration.

Though usually shorter than the Arrowauks, the Caribs were strong and muscular, active and lithe. To our eyes their appearance would have been anything but pleasing. In their cheeks and ears they made deep incisions, which were rendered conspicuous by being stained black; their faces and bodies were painted red with annotto, and round their eyes they were distinguished by circles of black and white. Some of the greater dandies pierced the cartilage of the nose, and inserted therein the bone of a fish, a piece of tortoise shell, or a parrot's feather. Instead of shells they strung together the teeth of their enemies slain in battle, whenever such could be obtained, and wore them round their arms and legs. Their arrows were usually poisoned, and when attacking an enemy by night the arrows were often tipped with cotton dipped in oil and set alight, in order to fire the dwellings they assailed. When a male child was born it was sprinkled with some drops of the father's blood, and as the child grew older it was if possible anointed with the fat of a slaughtered Arrowauk. When the boy entered manhood he had to undergo excruciating tortures in order to prove his prowess and claim to be accounted a warrior. They were not unskillful in the few arts with which they were conversant; they wove cotton and dyed it of various colors, red being the favorite color of the Caribs; they made pottery and burned it in a rough kiln, the shapes of some of their vessels being artistic and pleasing. They were particularly clever in weaving baskets of palmetto leaves, an art still retained by the Caribs of Dominica and St. Vincent, whose beautifully dyed and woven baskets are fashioned with such cunning that they will even hold water. Like the Arrowauks, they believed in future states of bliss or woe. In the former the braves were to enjoy supreme felicity with their wives and captives, while the spirits of cowards were to be banished eternally beyond the mountains, and doomed to everlasting toil in captivity to the Arrowauks. In every hut there was an altar made of banana leaves and reeds, on which they placed the earliest fruits and choice viands. Demons and evil spirits were dreaded and worshiped, and sacrifices offered to them by the hands of their Boyez, or magicians, the worshipers on such occasions wounding themselves by instruments made of the teeth of the agouti.

We can picture the depredations caused by the incessant marauding of bands of these ferocious cannibals, and the terror they must have excited in the minds of the milder islanders. Peter Martyr tells us that in his time alone more than five thousand men had been taken from the island of Sancti

Johannis to be eaten. Even after the Caribs had abandoned cannibalism they continued a fierce and desperate people, shunned and dreaded by Arrowauks and Europeans alike, and when cannibalism had ceased to be an everyday matter it would break out every now and then when occasion arose. The establishment of Spanish rule and the disappearance of the Arrowauks must have been the main factors in the decline of cannibalism, but before such was the case the Caribs seem to have given up the practice in some places. Thus Herrera says that "those of St. Croix and Dominica were greatly addicted to predatory excursions, hunting men," but not long before he wrote the Caribs of Dominica had eaten a poor monk, "and he so disagreed with them that many died, and that for a time they left off eating human flesh, making expeditions instead to carry off cows and mares."

When the English began to settle in the smaller Antilles they found the still unconquered Caribs a formidable obstacle peace, and they must have been a difficulty to be reckoned with till the close of the seventeenth century at least.

It is difficult to judge what were the number of the inhabitants of the islands at the time of the discovery. In 1495, when the Indians of Hispaniola rose against Columbus, according to the Spaniards, the number who revolted was a hundred thousand. Some authors place the native population of Hispaniola as high as three millions. It must have been impossible for the invaders to have formed any accurate computation of the number of inhabitants in countries so mountainous and impenetrable as were the larger Antilles. However, all accounts agree that the Indians were very numerous, and Las Casas describes the islands as "abounding with inhabitants, as an anthill with ants."

It seems extraordinary how so numerous a people could have been exterminated in so comparatively short a time. Oppression and cruelty alone could not have succeeded in wiping them out so completely. The Caribs were treated with greater severity than the Arrowauks, and their numbers were small in comparison with their less warlike neighbors, and yet the race survives to this day in Dominica and St. Vincent. Probably there was an inherent weakness in the race itself that tended to its destruction. They were timid and vicious, and timidity and vice are qualities that must hasten the disappearance of any people. Famine and disease seem to have been the chief factors in blotting out the Arrowauks. In Hispaniola the Indians, hoping to rid themselves of the voracious Spaniards, refused any longer to sow any crops. The Spaniards do not seem to have suffered as was expected, but in a few months no less than a third of the number of Indians in that island are said to have perished from starvation. But in 1518, according to Herrera, a scourge appeared in the Greater Antilles that almost desolated them. We know how great are the ravages of any imported disease among barbarians.

In our own days the natives of Fiji were swept off in thousands by so comparatively mild a distemper as measles: we can therefore understand how terrible must have been the ravages of so fatal an illness as smallpox, which was then first introduced from Europe. Even at the present day it is dreaded, but at that time it was twenty times more deadly and dreadful than now. The Indians were swept off in crowds, and the islands were almost depopulated. The mortality was increased by the miserable sufferers flinging themselves into the streams and rivers to seek relief from the burning fever that consumed them. Granting that the great majority of the Indians succumbed from disease and famine, the remainder of a people deficient in stamina might easily have dwindled away under the conditions then existing. Labor was odious to them, and that in the mines proved very fatal. The pearl fisheries also caused much mortality. These were chiefly worked by Indians from the Bahamas, who were expert divers and able to remain long under water; but so little care was taken of the men that they gradually died off, and, as the Bahama Islands had been entirely depopulated, it was impossible to supply their places.

Of course, the cruelty experienced, from their conquerors was one among other causes of the disappearance of the Arrowauks, but if the Indians were so numerous, it would be contrary to experience that oppression alone would so soon have exterminated such a multitude, in islands of such considerable area and so inaccessible to invaders.

Part II

The Physical Geography of the West Indies[2]

I.—THE FAUNA OF THE ANTILLES: MAMMALS.

The study of the geographical distribution of plants and animals has revealed facts almost as enigmatical as the origin of life itself. Water barriers, as broad as that of the Atlantic, have not prevented the spontaneous spread of some species, while others limit their habitat to narrowly circumscribed though not geographically isolated regions.

Tapirs are found both in the Amazon Valley and on the Malay Peninsula; the

[2] By Felix Leopold Oswald.

brook trout of southern New Zealand are identical with those of the Austrian Alps. Oaks and *Ericacea* (heather plants) cover northern Europe from the mouth of the Seine to the sources of the Ural; then suddenly cease, and are not found anywhere in the vast Siberian territories, with a north-to-south range rivaling that of all British North America.

But still more remarkable is the zoological contrast of such close neighborhood countries as Africa and Madagascar, or Central America and the West Indian archipelago. The Madagascar virgin woods harbor no lions, leopards, hyenas, or baboons, but boast not less than thirty-five species of mammals unknown to the African continent, and twenty-six found nowhere else in the world.

Of a dozen different kinds of deer, abundant in North America as well as in Asia and Europe, not a single species has found its way to the West Indies. The fine mountain meadows of Haiti have originated no antelopes, no wild sheep or wild goats.

In the Cuban sierras, towering to a height of 8,300 feet, there are no hill foxes. There are caverns—subterranean labyrinths with countless ramifications, some of them—but no cave bears or badgers, no marmots or weasels even, nor one of the numerous weasel-like creatures clambering about the rock clefts of Mexico. The magnificent coast forests of the Antilles produce wild-growing nuts enough to freight a thousand schooners every year, but—almost incredible to say—the explorers of sixteen generations have failed to discover a single species of squirrels.

The Old-World tribes of our tree-climbing relatives are so totally different from those of the American tropics that Humboldt's traveling companion, Bonplant, renounced the theory of a unitary center of creation (or evolution), and maintained that South America must have made a separate though unsuccessful attempt to rise from lemurs to manlike apes and men. Of such as they are, Brazil alone has forty-eight species of monkeys, and Venezuela at least thirty.

How shall we account for the fact that not one of the large West Indian islands betrays a vestige of an effort in the same direction?

More monkey-inviting forests than those of southern Haiti cannot be found in the tropics, but not even a marmoset or squirrel- monkey accepted the invitation. In an infinite series of centuries not one pair of quadrumana availed itself of the chance to cross a sea gap, though at several points the mainland approaches western Cuba within less than two hundred miles — about half the distance that separates southern Asia from Borneo, where fourhanders of all sizes and colors compete for the products of the wilderness, and, ac- cording to Sir Philip Maitland, the " native women avoid the coast jungles for fear of meeting Mr. Darwin's grandfather."

The first Spanish explorers of the Antilles were, in fact, so amazed at the apparently complete absence of quadrupeds that their only explanation was a conjecture that the beasts of the forest must have been exterminated by order of some native potentate, perhaps the great Kubla Khan, whose possessions they supposed to extend east- ward from Lake Aral to the Atlantic. The chronicle of Diego Columbus says positively that San Domingo and San Juan Bautista (Porto Rico) were void of mammals, but afterward modifies that statement by mentioning a species of rodent, the hutia, or bush rat, that annoyed the colonists of Fort Isabel, and caused them to make an appropriation for importing a cargo of cats.

Bush rats and moles were, up to the end of the sixteenth century, the only known indigenous quadrupeds of the entire West Indian archipelago, for the "Carib dogs," which Valverde saw in Jamaica, were believed to have been brought from the mainland by a horde of man-hunting savages.

But natural history has kept step with

the advance of other sciences, and the list of undoubtedly aboriginal mammals on the four main islands of the Antilles is now known to comprise more than twenty species. That at least fifteen of them escaped the attention of the Spanish Creoles is as strange as the fact that the Castilian cattle barons of Upper California did not suspect the existence of precious metals, though nearly the whole bonanza region of the San Joaquin Valley had been settled before the beginning of the seventeenth century. But the conquerors of the Philippines even overlooked a variety of elephants that roams the coast jungles of Mindanao.

Eight species of those West Indian incognito mammals, it is true, are creatures of a kind which the Spanish zoologists of Valverde's time would probably have classed with birds — bats, namely, including the curious Vespertilio molossus, or mastiff bat, and several varieties of the owl-faced Chilonycteris, that takes wing in the gloom preceding a thunderstorm, as well as in the morning and evening twilight, and flits up and down the coast rivers with screams that can be heard as plainly as the screech of a paroquet. The Vespertilio scandens of eastern San Domingo has a peculiar habit of flitting from tree to tree, and clambering about in quest of insects, almost with the agility of a flying squirrel. There are times when the moonlit woods near Cape Rafael seem to be all alive with the restless little creatures; that keep up a clicking chirp, and every now and then gather in swarms to contest a tempting find, or to settle some probate court litigation. San Domingo also harbors one species of those prototypes of the harpies, the fruit-eating bats. It passes the daylight hours in hollow trees, but becomes nervous toward sunset and apt to betray its hiding place by an impatient twitter — probably a collocution of angry comments on the length of time between meals. The moment the twilight deepens into gloom the chatterers flop out to fall on the next mango orchard and eat away like mortgage brokers. They do not get fat — champion gluttons rarely do — but attain a weight of six ounces, and the Haitian darkey would get even with them after a manner of their own if their prerogatives were not protected by the intensity of their musky odor. The above-mentioned hutia rat appears to have immigrated from some part of the world where the shortness of the summer justified the accumulation of large reserve stores of food, and under the influence of a hereditary hoarding instinct it now passes its existence constructing and filling a series of subterranean granaries. Besides, the females build nurseries, and all these burrows are connected by tunnels that enable their constructors to pass the rainy season under shelter. They gather nuts, belotas (a sort of sweet acorns), and all kinds of cereals, and with their penchant for appropriating roundish wooden objects on general principles would probably give a Connecticut nutmeg peddler the benefit of the doubt.

They also pilfer raisins, and a colony of such tithe collectors is a formidable nuisance, for the hutia is a giant of its tribe, and attains a length of sixteen inches, exclusive of the tail. It is found in Cuba, Haiti, Jamaica, Porto Rico, Antigua,

Trinidad, the Isle of Pines, Martinique, and two or three of the southern Bahama Islands, and there may have been a time when it had the archipelago all to itself. The Lucayans had a tradition that their ancestors found it on their arrival from the mainland, and in some coast regions of eastern Cuba it may still be seen basking in the sunlight —

"Sole sitting on the shore of old romance,"

and wondering if there are any larger mammals on this planet.

Its next West Indian congener is the Jamaica rice rat, and there are at least ten species of mice, all clearly distinct from any Old- World rodent, though, it is barely possible that some of them may have stolen a ride on Spanish trading vessels from Central America.

Water-moles burrow in the banks of several Cuban rivers, and two genera of aquatic mammals have solved the problem of survival : the bayou porpoise and the manatee, both known to the Creoles of the early colonial era, and vaguely even to the first discoverers, since Columbus himself alludes to a " sort of mermaids (sirenas) that half rose from the water and scanned the boat's crew with curious eyes."

Naturally the manatee is, indeed, by no means a timid creature, but bitter experience has changed its habits since the time when the down-town sportsmen of Santiago used to start in sailboats for the outer estuary and return before night with a week's supply of manatee meat. The best remaining hunting grounds are the reed shallows of Samana Bay (San Domingo) and the deltas of the

Haiti swamp rivers. Old specimens are generally as wary as the Prybilof fur seal that dive out of sight at the first glimpse of a sail; still, their slit-eyed youngsters are taken alive often enough, to be kept as public pets in many town ponds, where they learn to come to a whistle and waddle ashore for a handful of cabbage leaves.

Fish otters have been caught in the lagoons of Puerto Principe (central Cuba) and near Cape Tiburon, on the south coast of San Domingo, the traveler Gerstaecker saw a kind of "bushy-tailed dormouse, too small to be called a squirrel."

But the last four hundred years have enlarged the list of indigenous mammals in more than one sense, and the Chevalier de Saint-Mery should not have been criticised for describing the bush dog of Haiti as a "canis Hispaniolanus." Imported dogs enacted a declaration of independence several centuries before the revolt of the Haitian slaves, and their descendants have become as thoroughly West Indian as the Franks have become French. A continued process of elimination has made the survivors climate-proof and self-supporting, and above all they have ceased to vary; Nature has accepted their modified type as wholly adapted to the exigencies of their present habitat. And if it is true that all runaway animals revert in some degree to the characteristics of their primeval relatives, the ancestor of the domestic dog would appear to have been a bush-tailed, brindle-skinned, and black-muzzled brute, intermittently gregarious, and combining the burrowing propensity of the fox with the co-operative hunting penchant of the wolf.

Fourteen years of bushwhacker warfare have almost wholly ex- terminated the half -wild cattle of the Cuban sierras, but the bush dog has come to stay. The yelping of its whelps can be heard in thou- sands of jungle woods and mountain ravines, both of Cuba and Haiti, and no variety of thoroughbreds will venture to follow these renegades into the penetralia of their strongholds. Sergeant Esterman, who shared the potluck of a Cuban insurgent camp in the capacity of a gunsmith, estimates the wild-dog population of the province of Santiago alone at half a million, and predicts that in years to come their raids will almost preclude the possibility of profitable cattle- breeding in eastern Cuba.

Still, the perro pelon, or " tramp dog,"

as the Creoles call the wolfish cur, is perhaps a lesser evil, where its activity has tended to check the over-increase of another assisted immigrant. Three hundred years ago West Indian sportsmen began to import several breeds of Spanish rabbits, and with results not always foreseen by the agricultural neighbors of the experimenters. Rabbit meat, at first a luxury, soon became an incumbrance of the provision markets, and finally unsalable at any price. Every family with a dog or a trap- setting boy could have rabbit stew for dinner six times a week, and load their peddlers with bundles of rabbit skins.

The burrowing coneys threatened to undermine the agricultural basis of support, when it was learned that the planters of the Fort Isabel district (Haiti) had checked the evil by forcing their dogs to live on raw coney meat. The inexpensiveness of the expedient recommended its general adoption, and the rapidly multiplying quadrupeds soon found that "there were others." The Spanish hounds, too, could astonish the census reporter where their progeny was permitted to survive, and truck farmers ceased to complain.

In stress of circumstances the persecuted rodents then took refuge in the highlands, where they can still be seen scampering about the grassy dells in all directions, and the curs of the coast plain turned their attention to hutia venison and the eggs of the chaparral pheasant and other gallinaceous birds. On the seacoast they also have learned to catch turtles and subdivide them, regardless of antivivisection laws.

How they can get a business opening through the armor of the larger varieties seems a puzzle, but the canis rutilus of the Sunda Islands overcomes even the dog-resisting ability of the giant tortoise, and in Sumatra the bleaching skeletons of the victims have often been mistaken for the mementos of a savage battle.

Near Bocanso in southeastern Cuba the woods are alive with capuchin monkeys, that seem to have escaped from the wreck of some South American trading vessel and found the climate so congenial that they proceeded to make themselves at home, like the ring-tailed colonists of Fort Sable, in the Florida Everglades. The food supply may not be quite as abundant as in the equatorial birthland of their species, but that disadvantage is probably more than offset by the absence of tree-climbing carnivora.

Millions of runaway hogs roam the coast swamps of all the larger Antilles, and continue to multiply like our American pension claimants. The hunters of those jungle woods, indeed, must often smile to remember the complaint of the early settlers that the pleasure of the chase in the West Indian wilderness was modified by the scarcity of four-footed game, and in the total number (as distinct from the number of species) of wild or half-wild mammals Cuba and Haiti have begun to rival the island of Java.

II.—BIRDS

The abundance of birds on the four largest islands of the West Indian archipelago, where indigenous mammals are almost limited to rodents and bats, has often suggested the conjecture that the ancestors of those islanders must have been immigrants from the east coasts of the American mainland; and that theory seems to be confirmed by two facts: the identity, or similarity, of numerous Mexican and West Indian species, and the circumstance that those analogies include so many swift-winged birds.

There are no woodpeckers in the forests of the Antilles, and only two species of large gallinaceous birds, but a prodigious variety of pigeons, swallows, finches, and crows. The *alcedos* (kingfishers) are scarce, but the blackbirds so numerous that some of the countless species seem to claim a South American and even transatlantic ancestry.

CROWN PIGEON

The restless *estornino* of the Cuban highland forests, for instance, might be mistaken for a varnished starling, resembling the *Sturnus vulgaris* of western

Europe in everything but the more brilliant luster of its plumage. The curious *codornilla,* or dove quail, too, has its nearest relatives on the other side of the Atlantic, in Syria, Arabia, and the foothills of the Atlas. It builds its nest on the ground and, judging from its appearance, would seem to form a connecting link between the doves and small *gallinæ;* but its wings are those of a pigeon, and with the assistance of a, northeast gale may possibly have carried it across the ocean.

In studying the geographical distribution of animals, we may estimate the prevalence of special genera by the number of their varieties, or by the aggregate sum of individuals, and in the latter sense the migratory pigeons of our forest States once nearly outnumbered all the other birds of

North America, though the family is limited to five or six species. But in the West Indies the *Columbidæ* predominate in both respects. Cuba is a country of wild pigeons as preeminently as South Africa is a land of pachyderms and Madagascar of night monkeys. The *Columba leucocephala* (a congener of our ringdove) inhabits the mountain forests in countless swarms, and at the end of the rainy season visits grainfields in such numbers that hundreds are sometimes captured in nets, by means of corn scattered along the furrows.

A closely allied variety is found in San Domingo, where in many upland regions a darkey, equipped with a shotgun and a supply of gunpowder, can dispense with agriculture and raise a family of anthropoids on pigeon pies and *tortillas,* compounded from the grain found in the crops of his victims.

But the *tittyblang* (*tête-blanc*) has scores of smaller and larger cousins, culminating in the Cuban primate of the family, the splendid *paloma real,* with its coronet of pearl-gray plumes and dark-blue wings.

Ducks, too, must number some twenty West Indian species, and one kind of wild geese often obliged the rice planters to employ mounted sharpshooters, who galloped up and down the long dikes, yelling blasphemies, and every now and then enforcing their quotations with a handful of buckshot. But, for all that, the planter could think himself lucky to gather a sixty-per-cent harvest of the total produce, for experience soon enabled the long-necked depredators to estimate the target range of the *cazador* within a dozen yards and take wing in the nick of time, only to resume their feast at the other end of the plantation. A long-continued process of natural selection has also modified the habits of numerous species of West Indian parrots.

CRESTED CURASSOW.

PORTO RICO PARRAKEET.

Four hundred years ago, when Fernan Oviedo superintended the placer mines of Haiti, *loris* were so abundant and tame that his assistants often amused themselves prowling about a thicket of berry bushes and capturing the chattering visitors by means of a common ring net.

VERVAIN HUMMING BIRD AND NEST.

Nestlings could be taken from every hollow tree, and often from the thatchwork of deserted Indian cabins; but the overconfident specimens came to grief, and the survivors have learned to give the Caucasian varieties of the *Simia destructor* a wide berth. They raise their young in the cavities of the tallest forest trees, and approach human habitations only at dawn of day and sometimes during the noonday heat, when Creoles can be relied upon to indulge in a siesta nap. In reliance on their protective colors, gray parrakeets frequent the dead timber of the coffee plantations, while the leaf-green Amazon parrot sticks to leaf trees.

"When they alight on a dry branch," says Captain Gosse, in his Jamaica chronicle, "their emerald hue is conspicuous and affords a fair mark for the gunner, but in a tree of full foliage their color proves an excellent concealment. They seem aware of this, and their sagacity prompts them to rely on it for protection. Often we hear their voices proceeding from a certain tree, or have marked the descent of a flock, but on proceeding to the spot, though the eye has not wandered from it, we cannot discover an individual; we go close to the tree, but all is silent; we institute a careful survey of every part with the eye, to detect the slightest motion, or the form of a bird among the leaves, but in vain, and we begin to think that they have stolen off unperceived, but on throwing a stone into the tree a dozen voices burst forth into cry, and as many green birds dart forth upon the wing."

The gorgeous macaws, on the other hand, seem to owe their color contrasts to sexual selection. "Ya son vencidos los pavos de India"—"That does beat a Hindostan peacock"—exclaimed King Ferdinand, when Columbus introduced those most splendid products of the American tropics.

Nor can the exigencies of protection have evolved the glaring colors of the West Indian hornbill. The *toco* (toucan), as the Cubans call the yellow-billed species, can be descried from a distance of two hundred yards, and is, indeed, not anxious to be admired at close range. Old specimens get as wary as mountain ravens, but, like crows, become ridiculously tame in captivity, and will follow their proprietors with loud croaks, every now and then opening their lunchtrap to indicate their desire for refreshment. They are, on the whole, the hardiest of all tropical birds, and can weather the winters of our coast towns as far north as Wilmington, in open-air cages, owing perhaps to their habit of extending their excursions to the high mountain ranges of their native land.

THE SMALLEST BIRD.

Economical Nature rarely wastes the gift of song on a bird of bright plumage, but it is less easy to understand why so many feathered beauties should have been afflicted with harsh and positively repulsive voices. The horrid screams of the peacocks, guinea hens, and macaws can hardly be supposed to charm their mates, and are too easily recognized to deter their natural enemies. But the roars (there is no more adequate word) of some species of hornbills would almost seem intended to serve the latter purpose. "The voice of the *Buceros bicornis*" says Wallace, "can be plainly heard at a distance of a mile, so that the amazement of travelers visiting its haunts seems explicable enough. Its screams may be described as something between the bray of a jackass and the shriek of a locomotive, and are not surpassed in power by any sound that an animal is capable of making. They re-echo through the hills to such a degree that it is difficult to assign the noise to a bird, and are sometimes kept up so continuously as to become absolutely unbearable."

The condor and the harpy eagle have not found their way across the Caribbean Sea, but the West Indies boast three varieties of fish eagles, several species of mountain falcons, and a curious singing owl, the *oriya*, that chants its serenades in the plaintive strain of the whip-poor-will, and is dreaded by the Porto Rico darkeys as a bird of ill-omen:

"Grita l'oriya: Veuga amigo,
Venga coumigo a mi patria,
Venga te-digo!"

Small hooting owls abound, and there are four species of sparrow hawks, one of them not much larger than a finch.

It is probably the smallest bird of prey, and there is no doubt that one species of West Indian humming bird is the smallest bird on earth, the *Vervain colibri*, of Jamaica, that hides its nest under an orange leaf, and, though an insect-eater, could be easily overpowered by an able-bodied bumblebee. In beauty some of the south Cuban species rival those of the Amazon Valley, and frequent every flowering shrub from the jungles of the coast lands to the highland meadows of the Sierra Maestra. In Haiti there are parklike plateaus where they often appear in swarms at a time of the year when the forests of the foothills are drenched by the afternoon cloudbursts of the rainy season, and on some of the smaller Antilles they are seen only during the flowering period of special plants.

In the solitudes of the Morne Range (San Domingo) mountain ravens rear their brood in the crevices of steep rocks, and fiercely attack birds of prey, not excepting the black-crested eagle, that now and then visits the sierras in quest of conies. But the winged constables of the highlands rarely leave their mountain reservation. Of Abd-el-Wahab, the Arabian heretic, it used to be said that "Mohammedan zealots shrank in affright from his superior fanaticism," and on the midway terraces of the Dominican sierras the persecution mania of the giant crow yields to that of the great shrike, the *Lanius rufus*, that operates pairwise and assails all winged comers with absolutely reckless courage.

The raven of the Mornes seems to be identical with the cosmopolitan forager that is found in the uplands of the eastern continent from the bleak summit regions of the Hindu-Kush to the sierras of Portugal, and from the Atlas to the Norwegian Alps; but there are several exclusively West

Indian species of the genus *Corvus,* including a steel-blue rook that flits about the Cuban coffee plantations and has a curious habit of perching on a stump and talking to itself in a sort of croaking chuckle for half hours together.

The *gallinæ,* as might be expected from their limited wing-power, are well represented in the number of individuals, rather than of species. Turkeys, though abundant in the coast forests of Central

THE CARIBBEAN ALBATROSS.

America, are not found wild in any part of the West Indies, where the perennial presence of berries would be as inviting as the absence of foxes.

In the mountains some species of curassow have, however, developed into a stately game bird, the *Oreophasis niger,* or highland "pheasant," that lays a dozen large eggs, and in its courtship season becomes so infatuated that it can be approached and killed with a common walking-stick. The consequent persecution has made it rather scarce in famine-stricken Cuba, but in Haiti it can still be seen in troops of a dozen or more, scratching up the dry leaves of the sierra forests, or pecking at insect-haunted shrubs, exactly like a flock of Tennessee turkeys.

There are also several varieties of true pheasants, and two species of quail (besides the above-mentioned *codornilla*), and in eastern Cuba numerous barnyard chickens have taken to the woods and become so shy that it seems a puzzle how their ancestors in the coast range of Burmah could ever be captured and domesticated. They still practice polygamy, combined with a system of co-operative housekeeping, to judge from the number of eggs that are often found in one nest. At the approach of an unfeathered biped the hen bird takes wing with a screech, and is apt to vanish for the rest of that day. The roosters are rarely seen, their glaring colors having faded into more protective shades of olive and brown, but at dawn of day their shrill reveille can be heard from afar in the heart of the pathless jungle woods.

III.—REPTILES AND FISHES.

The present fauna of our planet includes many varieties of mammals and reptiles, and a few kinds of birds, that are found only on certain islands—a fact which seemed rather to justify the once universal belief in the origin of species by separate acts of creation.

A different theory of explanation has, however, been suggested by the discovery of fossil remains, proving the former existence of closely allied forms on continents where their battle for existence had to be fought against beasts of prey and competitors for a limited food supply.

The supposed products of an island genesis by the fiat of supernatural agencies, demanding recognition in mental penance and the payment of tithes, may thus be simply animal Crusoes, favored by the positive or negative advantages of their surroundings.

The dodo, in its struggle for survival, would have had no chance against South American tiger-cats. Not one of the twenty-odd species of Madagascar lemurs could have held its own against the competition of the African daylight monkeys.

Yet there was a time when night apes and large ground birds seem to have had things all their own way, the world over, and Central America may have afforded a chance for existence to several species of reptiles which at present are found only on the West Indian islands.

The Cuban bush tortoise (*Eniys nigra*) is found only in the forests of Santiago and Puerto Principe, and there only on the south coasts. It is the most sluggish creature of its genus, and does not seem to have had enterprise enough to crawl around the sand belt of Cape Maysi and colonize the jungles of the north side provinces. It is as helpless as a hedgehog, *minus* its bristles. The darkeys of the Cuban planters crack its armor with home-made hammers, and the *tortuga prieta,* or prieta, as they call it for short, forms a factor of holiday *menus* as frequently as 'possum pie in southern Georgia.

Swift-flowing rivers bear it away as they would a floating log, and it is wholly incredible that its ancestors should have crossed the Caribbean Sea in quest of a more congenial home; but it is possible enough that its eggs may have been ferried across on one of the driftwood islands which the Sumasinta River often tears from the coast swamps of southern Mexico and carries into the current of the Gulf Stream. The evolution of the South American giant cats was probably the death warrant of its continental relatives, but in Cuba it had no four-footed enemies except the *hutia,* or jungle rat, that now and then destroys its eggs.

IGUANA.

An equally favored islander is the grayish-yellow rock lizard, abounding in the uplands of Cuba and Haiti. The lizard-killing cranes of Honduras have not found their way to the Antilles, and the *lagartilla* still basks in the sun that once smiled upon the indolence of the naked Lucayans.

The *toco,* or Cuban hornbill, however, devours small reptiles of all sorts, and the West Indian tree lizards have become almost as nimble as squirrels. They dodge behind branches and wait to ascertain the origin of every flitting shadow, but from imminent danger save themselves by a swift descent, followed by a bold leap into the thickets of the underbrush. Their courtship is quite as grotesque as that of the strutting bush pheasants. The males will swing their heads up and down and puff up their throat-bags till their skin seems on the point of disruption, while the objects of their rivalry sit blinking, reluctant to risk an open manifestation of preference. Some gorgeously beautiful varieties are found in Jamaica: greenish-blue, with a metallic luster, and rows of bright crimson spots, as if the design of protective colors had been patterned after the flower shrubs of the tropics.

The word *iguana* is of Mexican origin, and rarely used in the Spanish West Indies, but the animal itself is—for culinary purposes, though the Haitian negroes do not go quite as far as the mongrels of Yucatan, where iguana farmers fatten the defenseless reptiles with cornmeal, in wickerwork baskets, that are brought to market as a New England poultry fancier would fetch in a crateful of spring chickens. But, prejudice aside, there is no harm in an iguana fricassee; the meat is white and insipid, but takes the flavor of every spice, and is far more digestible than such hyperborean delicacies as. fried eels and pork fritters. There are two species—one in eastern Cuba, with spines all the way down to its tail-tip, and in Haiti a smaller one, with a smoother tail, but with an exaggerated throat-bag and wattles like a turkey gobbler.

Lagartos vastecos, or "tree alligators," the Cuban Creoles call the scampering forest dwellers, that attain a length of four feet, and can stampede foreigners by leaping to terra firma with an *aplomb* that scatters the dry leaves in all directions. If chased, they will take to water like frogs. They are first-class swimmers, their throat-bag serving the purpose of a float, and once in the ripple of the stream are hard to keep in sight, as they have a trick of keeping their legs close to the body and navigating by means of their submerged tails. Like the rainbow hues of the coryphene (miscalled dolphin), the bright colors of the iguana soon fade after death, and the shriveled greenish-brown specimens of our taxidermists give no idea of the appearance of the living animal in the sunlight of its native land. The *Iguana tuherculata* (eastern Cuba) is velvet-green above, with saffron flanks, ringed with blue, black, and brown stripes, and the pet specimens, basking on the porch of a coffee planter, can challenge comparison with the paroquets that flutter about the eaves of the outbuildings like swifts around a martin box.

FER-DE-LANCE.

Cuba has also acclimatized a horned frog, and one species of those curious half-lizards whose shapes may have suggested the dragon fables of antiquity. The "basilisk" (*Cyclura carinata*) is only half a yard long, but can erect its crest and raise its pronged tail in a manner that will make a dog leap back in affright. It has no goiter-bag, but the skin of its throat is elastic, and can be made to swell out like that of the East Indian cobra, while its multiplex spines vibrate ominously. The little monster is, nevertheless, one of the most harmless reptiles of the tropics, and subsists on succulent leaves, with occasional *entremets* of small grubs and insects. In that case, however, Nature has rather overdone its efforts at protective ugliness, and the Creoles kill the poor simulator of terrors as the Mexican rustics would a horned toad.

A plurality of the zoological immigrants of the West Indies seem to have come from Mexico, and it is a suggestive fact that the number of reptiles steadily decreases from west to east. Cuba, with its western headland approaching the east coast of Yucatan, thus came in for a lion's share of lizards, tortoises, and ophidians.

Haiti, though only one fourth smaller, experienced a seventy-five-per-cent discount, and all natives and travelers agree on the *curiosum* that there is *not a single species of serpent* on the island of Porto Rico. Trinidad, with an area of only fifteen hundred square miles, but laved by the giant current of the Orinoco, boasts twenty-eight species of land serpents, besides several pythons and swamp vipers. The Trinidad museum of venomous ophidians does not, however, include the dreaded fer-de-lance, which infests the woods near Samana Bay on the south coast of San Domingo. The *Bothrops lanceolatus* is larger than a rattlesnake, and its bite, though not always fatal, causes fearful inflammation, but its aggressive disposition has been greatly exaggerated. Like most venomous serpents, it is a sluggish brute, relying on its ability to crouch motionless till its prey comes in range, then get in a snap bite and shrink back to wait till the virus begins to take effect, and the victim, in its fever spasms, betrays its helplessness by those eccentricities of conduct which are apt to be misinterpreted by the dupes of the "serpent-charm" superstition.

The fer-de-lance is found also on the islands of Martinique and Santa Lucia, where the natives counteract its virus with a decoction of jungle hemlock, and the basis of its grewsome reputation seems to be the fact that it does not warn the intruders of its haunts, after the manner of the cobra or the rattlesnake, but flattens its coils and, with slightly vibrating tail, awaits events. If the unsuspecting traveler should show no sign of hostile intent he may be allowed to pass unharmed within two yards of the coiled matador, but a closer approach is apt to be construed as a challenge, and the *vivoron*, suddenly rearing its ugly head, may scare the trespasser into some motion of self-defense—he may lift his foot or brandish his stick in a menacing manner. If he does he is lost. The lower coils will expand, bringing the business end, neck and all, a few feet nearer; the bead "points," like a leveled rifle, then darts forward with electric swiftness, guided by an unerring instinct for the selection of the least-protected parts of the body.

And the vindictive brute is ready to repeat its bite. For a moment it rears back, trembling with excitement, and, if felled by a blow of its victim's stick, will snap away savagely at stumps and stones, or even, like a wounded panther, at its own body.

A very curious adaptation of means to ends in the modification of the virus is its swiftly fatal effect on birds. A stricken child, though half crazed with fear, may run a distance of three miles before paralysis begins to impede its motions; a squirrel will escape to its nest in the top of the tree, only to come forth again and topple down in its delirium; but a bird drops as if he had swallowed a dose of prussic acid.

BUTTERFLY FISH.

Serpent virus is specifically a bird poison; in other words, it acts instantaneously in cases where a few moments' delay would defeat the purpose of the snap bite. Wounded rodents will not run very far and can be relied upon to come out of their holes; but a bitten bird, unless promptly paralyzed, would fly out of sight and drop in distant thickets, beyond the ken of its destroyer. And of all bird-killing reptiles the fer-de-lance is the most destructive. The Spaniards have varied its bill of fare by importing the wherewithal of an occasional rabbit stew, but during the preceding ages it had to subsist on poultry, like a popular circuit preacher—the hutia rat having developed a talent for avoiding its haunts.

The alleged *horror naturalis* of serpents is perhaps not more deep-rooted than the aversion to cats; at all events, the West Indians have overcome it sufficiently to prefer rat-killing snakes to tabbies. In thousands of rancho cabins a pet serpent of the genus *coluber* may be seen gliding noiselessly along the rafters, or slip through the crack of a floor plank to reach the penetralia of the basement, where the death shriek of rodents soon after announces the result of its activity. Aristocratic creoles relegate it to their stables, but the tenants of numerous backwood *casuchas* furnish it a cotton-stuffed bed box, and reward its services with a weekly dish of milk. There are several species of large river serpents, and one true boa, the *Cuban matapollos*, or chicken-killer, that attains a length of eighteen feet, and has been known to use its supernumerary coils for the purpose of cracking the ribs of a hound flying to the assistance of the barnyard rooster.

FLYING FISH (*Exocœtus volitans*); *FLYING GURNARD OR FLYING ROBIN* (Cephalacanthus volitans). *(From Baskett's Story of the Fishes.)*

In addition to the above-mentioned jungle tortoise there are several land turtles of the genus *chlemmys*, and thousands of chelidonians are annually caught on Samana Bay, southern Porto Rico, St. Vincent, the Isle of Pines, and the north coast of Matanzas, Cuba. Those of Santiago Bay have gradually been exterminated, but a large number of West Indian fishing waters are practically inexhaustible. A specialist like Agassiz might haul nondescripts from scores of Haitian coast rivers, and the angle fishers of the Cuban sierra brooks can hook an equally interesting reproduction of an Appalachian species.

"Some of our companions had to eke out a haul with crawfish," says the traveler Esterman, "but our own string of sundries included a puzzle for naturalists. We had caught some twenty brook trout, absolutely indistinguishable from the species found in the head waters of the Tennessee River. Where did they come from? Had they crossed the Gulf of Mexico and ascended the rapids of half a hundred rivers, or had Nature copied her own handiwork in such details as the small dark dots below each red spot, and the occasional breaks in the lines of the silver-white keel streaks?"

The perch of the forest rivers include several nest-building varieties, and the sportsmen of Kingston, Jamaica, often amuse themselves with target practice at a species of rock fish that come clear out of the water and bask, like coots, on the harbor cliffs.

With every mile farther south the number and variety of the finned aborigines become more infinite, and the fishermen of the estuary of San Juan de Porto Rico alone catch pompanos, mullets, cavalli, red snappers, chiquillos (a kind of sardelles), sea bass, dorados, skip-jack, angelfish, skate, ray, sheepshead, garfish, torpedo-fish, devilfish or giant ray, cobia, hogfish, croakers, shark, and coryphenes.

The tiger of the sea, the great white shark, occasionally visits the harbor waters of Cuba, and has been known to seize barefooted peons, surf-bathing horses in the next neighborhood of Morro Castle, and drag them under so suddenly that their companions were unable to account for their disappearance till the foam of the breakers became flecked with blood.

That champion of marine man-eaters is as smooth as a hypocrite, and hides its double row of horrible fangs under a slippery nose, while the little butterfly fish tries its best to disguise its helplessness with a crest of spiny fins. Its length rarely exceeds four inches, and it can be handled with impunity, but its spines are just rigid enough to entangle it in tufts of gulf weed, and in company of equally tiny sea horses and goldfish, it can often be seen in the aquariums of the Jamaica seaport towns.